GRUNT

OF

the

MÍNOTAUR

GRUNT

OF
the
MINOTAUR

Robin Richardson

INSOMNIAC PRESS

Library and Archives Canada Cataloguing in Publication

Richardson, Robin, 1985-
Grunt of the Minotaur / Robin Richardson.

Poems.
ISBN 978-1-55483-031-2

I. Title.

PS8635.I3338G78 2011   C811'.6   C2011-905340-3

The publisher gratefully acknowledges the support of
the Canada Council, the Ontario Arts Council,
and the Department of Canadian Heritage through the
Canada Book Fund.

Printed and bound in Canada

Insomniac Press
520 Princess Avenue, London, Ontario, Canada, N6B 2B8
www.insomniacpress.com

ONTARIO ARTS COUNCIL
CONSEIL DES ARTS DE L'ONTARIO

For Sean Stanley

Have you ever noticed how the more the world looks like a
bad oil painting, the more likely you are to say,
"My gad, isn't it gorgeous?"

Well, I've wrestled with reality for thirty-five years, Doctor,
and I'm happy to state I finally won out over it.
—Elwood P. Dowd

CONTENTS

HOW GODS ARE MADE

What was left between the teeth, crushed pearl
many coloured glass splints, made it difficult

to speak. The two girls, still alive, bobbed up
and down, splitting rock, moving further inland.

The town would be a simple matter, being too strong
to shake hands, they'd wave, mounted on horseback,

tattoos bared through veils, still scabbing,
further proof they were human. Though

sugarcane became them and the growing
girth of dirt made them pass like water over graves.

TEXT AND TAXIDERMY

The high brow ridge, streaked dark with eyelash,
is the hub of the world. It's alarming
how close to casual speech we perceive
these lips, though wax and glass encased.

I see it flattened out, bronze along the surface:

Hominid, hibiscus, sharp chipped rock, boar
or wildebeest, burrowing the thickness of a bush,
marsh, how the dark feet would one day weaken
– soft – and shrink.

Frequently we want the well-carved face,
fingers widening, clasped about the spear,
to obstruct, come out tempered
by a glint of life, shoulder close, holding
neck and other flesh to fold away.

WHEN PAYING VISITS OF CONDOLENCE

To courteously desire the deceased,
one should be dressed in silk,
be slight of word, coo, pretend to give a kiss
when sniffing the seasoned marrow.
Like a mule, brush the rug with suede,
tap the pound cake, clutch
pie, caramelized to hide the taste.
If foul play is suspected, flood the glass
with cognac, keep rumours to a hush.
The doorframe cramped with hands
and winter hats at hooks like hangmen. To lick
the velvet pouch, let a hand slip down
past the necktie, is the failure of a man
to keep his starched and eggshell grin in place.
Think not of flowerbeds, though far
and harmless. It's rude to couple
where the buried bruise the pebbled hills.

Retires from a Falling Out

Small moths taper, thaw a pale arm
to lift and come to life. Diplomat
lifts his joint, pulls quiet and burns.
He's all shoulder, states
his frame with reverence
for the high-backed chair. Lap
of crumpled slacks. He's not
for preaching. Peach pits
stacked and rolling at his feet, he
feels a breeze. Nodding curtain
curves causeway, cat lumps
herald-wise beside his loafers.
Runt he calls her, learns to listen
when she breathes as if she's singing.

Citing Dimensions of Mad and Mundane Counsel

Little is known of the Middle Ages,
though rococo chairs have long been
the common man's failing memory.

With clauses apt to tongue-tie,
take the walnut-panelled locks
from faces, torches

carried over textbook spines,
courtier or crooked brass basket
wove too tight to clasp the finger.

Or likewise fight the obligation
of an arm offered up in buttermilk
abduction. This is how duty implores,

intimated by the watch, tyranny
of tin and magnet, gentle in a kind
of ennui. Without the boastful

noble enemy of high official rank,
there's only task: talk to her, cook
the dining room drabble to a gold,

good-humoured wrap of conversation.
Afternoon is plain. Ten pages make
the brisk walk from Wagner's minor

chords to the low sliding grunt
of the Minotaur.

WHEN RETIRING FOR THE NIGHT

Appoint the various domestic disorders
to separate rooms. It's impossible to master
lights. Each separate occasion
rising for distinction in the lamp.

Keep the fire burning. Glad to wrap the heads
of guests in non-specific yellow gas. The gardener
may trip his shears: a finger lost and pointing
at your room. Ignore the creaking

wooden headboards, punctual shift
in temperature, with a book. The passage
may seem difficult, may be excused for
honest avails of sex or finger play.

This is how the mistress takes her nap, established
in the praises of useless conduct. She may wish
to part the brackets, politely printed
in a letter of introduction. Take the dusted

words to bed, acknowledge, politely, the beauty
of her guests. Though their husbands polish
themselves inside her and the windows
pout for want of her slightly parted petticoat.

Rawhide Citizenry

The hunter, with a flask of brandy, pines
for glass, the clear outline of a windowpane,

resumes his fight, footsteps of a bear
partially qualified by hailstorms, illusions
of civil law or the severity of rabbits nibbling
on a ruin's perch. With altered blades, copper
bullets built to splinter, the uncharacteristically
warm corpse still rummaging, clean scraped
by the Inuit scapula.

It is important to record the weak spots,
though all fall soft against the gun.

POINTED BLACK DROP SHADOW

The mind has exactly the same power as the hands;
not merely to grasp the world, but to change it.
–Colin Wilson

Colin Wilson would say it's the girl,
parapet, rolling shutters, single casement
window. With grieving gemstone, inch
by inch parallels like lymph nodes
twitching, unravelled in asymmetric folds.

There was a mug on the table, the girl's
rhombus step-cut emerald dipped like a biscuit
in milk, bit through by a fork-toothed
mouth and spat minced salad
on her brown braided pigtails.

She was spindly. Just now menstrual, a peach leaf
in her teeth, she smiled: cane chair, powder box
scoffed, shuddered. Nothing could be done.
The pelvis of this girl, turning worlds like
an Arab's flute, would have to do.

TO TRUSS A BIRD

Tie wings and thighs with garnish
to a single-minded bride. Adjust

her pastry hands, palms
out, wrists like ice picks

to catch the flavour of a crop or
ovum, green-scrubbed and leaking.

Her waist might sink,
fingers fold like domes

around the beak. Place her basting
in a diamond swathe, punctual

and subject to converse gaily
with the chef. She may wait

for dinner, patient in a salted sachet
or smoked artichoke negligee.

BLUE

Blue mountain, blue eyes; the youth's bluish
humming in monastic fields. Here he sees
the water, hears the humbling quiet of a drop.

Swans pass like shifting latitudes
East inches over and the Earth commiserates,
it's lost its place.

The youth yawns, not fit for this Pacific
prelude. Blue words mute, he thinks of black
instead. Shakes a mist from his boot.

The iris of an ocean makes its way through
gazers as they pass, possessed by repetition,
breaking wave on breaking wave.

Round O, open voice of coo as blue birds
break the clouds from their apparent
likenesses. Weather will not do.

The youth, not merely here, but strewn
in thought across the scene, resumes his hum –
lumbers slumped on wicker-woven grass.

Beyond the field is a forest, further still
plutonic bodies in their orbs. Beyond
the orbs the gods are marble nudes – contrapposto,

so the pedestals seem small beneath their feet.
Blue is their demeanour. Fixed figures
huddled. Though the water sings them, swans

renounce their names. The youth exits,
framed by low-hung stratus.
The scene conspires in his absence: blue.

MOVING PROBLEMATIC THROUGH A BRIDGE

Finding this: a bone, wind-scourged
picks of early man, present-day aluminum foil,
an axe and a novel decidedly too old

to follow. A pinch, handful, this old man's
ragged spade. Yes, he conceded. It was
out of date. In fall he broke his leg,

moved with a new fragile dexterity,
claimed the foibles of the land
his only friends.

SUBMISSION OF A ROSE'S NAKED FLINT

On her first day a girl may not process
the heads of mice, only carve the kitchen
stairs, embellish the cherub flowers of wood
relief. She may ready herself for waltzes
with the door's mocking bell tower steady
in idle. She's not to think us average, must
believe the walls depend upon a high-hanging
rake. Our prince is a pinch of clove, mirrors:
inferior blue disks of light. This way, unclothed,
in the crowfoot tub, she'll fill herself with fables,
her diaries aggrandizing.

Layman and the Lynching Tree

They passed, not walking, but stretched out
trembling through the green. Sawn
was the ground, lengthened with a twist
of drawstring. As if grass were wool, crickets
the cross-stitch of this kitchen window view.

Absorbed I watched them slump off lean
and preening for the glass, tender-dressed
and frosted at the shock of being hanged some two
hundred years ago. Vague, the chatter, occasional pitch
like something ticking. They would hone the wind.

Modest rising out around translucent limbs
humming something, hovering larynx, different from
the slightly parted fingers wrapped up in tapping
at the oak and copper cupboards. They fluttered
once, covered the room with dirt and resolution.

BLUE SHADE ALABASTER SKIN

With effort to regain control, noticing first
the flesh, next a ring of roast beef kneaded
at the kitchen table. Rusted stovetop raw
with salmonella. Maybe, whether or not
she knows it, she's almost boneless. Old
as the tuatara, marbled blue like maps of early
puddles. On her birch-arched chairs, obedient,
stalling for the gravy, botched by the black loose
nail hung like a shingle from her thumb.
There's order forged by pilgrims in her head.
The plates warmed, silverware set in slopes
of rank, wine at measured intervals to prove
the pulse still moves under the olive cotton
cardigan, worn specially for guests. Aged oak
floor, mistaken for a curve, unfortunate
imbalance of a step. We avoid laughter,
press the teeth to keep her thinking we don't notice.

GOYA'S SHARP-TOOTHED MUSES

Both hit the ground imploding.

Both are dust, boastful candidates for constellations.

Both bring Bibles to the fold, then talk of feet beneath
the bench.

Both ache waking.

Both take shelter, tear sheep's skin through a grind of
fists.

Both curt, bare, both ride with grizzlies in their teeth –
smiling.

Both are seamless where the blind man meets the
gutter with a thud.

Both know the study, slouched scalps in dim-lit
contract with the word.

Both will pull, pass as stallions through a panicked
mind.

The Quasi-Existence of Infants

Those gnats need little alarm.

Buoyant as firmly scraped olives,
rubbed with spirits to evoke the standard
succession of cries.

Valves vigilant as freight trains.

The failing of spine or finger wrapped
with gasps, gone grape then black.

Mute for language.

Will tilt their heads, parch drinking
lips with gulps of air for want
of mother's brandy.

On Being Shaded with a Foible

As if looks could lift the boundaries
of a Sunday room, take on
treetops across the garden.
She remarks on the frankness
of the street, closed quarters
of a drawing room, how far apart
two arms touching can seem.
She glazes conversations, states
instead the failing of a nose to help
compose a neighbour's face, how
cabinets irk, stall the taking up of plates
and silver spoons. She pictures
each gesture as if framed by twisted
pillars, scratching at the plate,
spoon too cold to mimic taste,
settles instead on the side-to-side
sway of a dying fire, spastic orange-
grazed cheeks, faint hovering
sense of something out of sight.
There's an oddness about the wording,
expressive of a single face, alert
in square-jawed curiosity.

THE TREATMENT OF NATURAL DISASTERS

Lying almost silver beneath the fallen
chandelier, as if her legs were light,
the shattered surface of her face
engraved and jade.

We'd watched her romp on the marble
floor's slight slant. She sang her veins
open in the earthquake's last beat, or at least
that's how we would tell it.

Fine china, crystal cups now dust that
cuts the palms. The soles of formal shoes,
generally dazzling, save the pain, the way
it inches inside. Still we walk about,

step as if the streams were string,
rewrite the invitations, intent that
superstition could undo the tangled lapse
of crystal in an evening gown.

Against the Moths

With Russian leather, the tailor expresses
a cold diddling schoolgirl. Gold is the lip,
cadmium, the little ring finger. He ties
a pouch to the belt, loose thread,
a hiccup in the stitching. Out
against the high brown leg, tightened belly.

He makes buttons from bones, so well
fondled that the needle's numb. Lace
on his table, a book of dirty jokes, pink
and black and yellow bodies. He dries the tips
of nipples, little clips to heal injured cotton. To cure
the suede of faded tapered hems.

In the drain there is a mangled nightie, the over-
washed linen wrapped around a pipe. *Some say
he killed her*, fastened her hair to the tassel
of a gown. He breathes like the hog, dresses
the mannequin and hums to drown the sound.

A Post-Industrial Eulogy

The brass handles became you, drawn down in July.
The aftermath is never as assured, well-placed
as the parlour flowers, perfectly arranged in tusk-white
domes. You opened your hands, your mouth, watched
the crosses marching, ushered by the twenty-some-odd
two-by-two procession. Trusted the past.

Red stripes of the barber wrapped like cherry
floss around a pole. At least he used his hands, letting
blood as he swiped bristles from a pale chin.

NOT KISSING IN ROMANTIC PLACES

It was a passing show, dismantled in June
by a dozen blue-faced masqueraders.

I didn't mind.

The empty round rooms where we restored
plaster faces: somber clown, stone waiter
and feather-clinging elephant.

We'd found it at night, overturned in the sea salt.

You fit perfectly between the eyes of an oversize mouse,
heavyset, slanted where the boxcars once slid
prohibited by rails.

Still, the sea lulled quiet a ring of painted metal swings.

MAY HAVE WALKED MORE SLOWLY

Horseflies forge a sphere, dim a pilgrim's
vision, huddling, holding out the light
in their armour. Pilgrim snares a blister
on the ridge, his boots broken by the heel,
soaking moss as scabs, ants as minced red
calluses. He dawdles, crossing tufts of rabbit,
ragweed, wind-smoothed stones, silver
as the crucifix against his sternum.
He fiddles as he walks; waltzes made
for planks of Paris birch. He'll play
a hymn when he arrives. Each chapel
painted Dulac like Elizabethan shrines.

BECOME A HUNTER

Become a hunter,
twelve days, eight hours
in the roots.

How the pheasant grimaces,
what it gains in the luxury
of a kitchen, cut, for instance,

by a girl engaged in garlic
paste, hard-crusted dough.
She considers your absence,

observes the game, knife
detached, skin loosened
at the upper joints.

Breastbone and wings
she wishes to secure with
packthread to her shoulders.

To find the hunter,
free her tongue, beaked
and genial, sport your bullet,

tree-scraped feathers
as she is laid, mace
and onion on your plate.

FALSE SKETCHES ON A BEDPOST

Hers was a yellow flag rousing back and forth
above the houses.

She wondered what, if anything, she'd forgotten –
the front door a tomb.

She yawned, shut her book, crying, "Yes, yes," and
why not wrap the pillow with her legs.

The boy could have been a field, flock
of birds. She thought of his beard,

about the thinness of her own fingers,
union of her thoughts and the climate

of her thighs. She tried, again,
to remember dull trifles of the day

threatening her pleasure. There was the street,
stifled pets, respectable neighbours sleeping.

"No," she cried, "this is not what I am for!"
The empty room, nightlight agreed,

speaking tulip till she came.

The Reluctance of a Psychic

She couldn't restrain herself, struck
an arm against the voices, speeches
flowing on, varied in their pitch, opinions,
the real-feeling chill of clairvoyance.

She could almost reach them, teetering
on ebb and flow, the ignorance
of Milton, spirit where the villain roused
attentively, could have been a snake, or worse,

a bird, lovestruck, warbling flightless
in its daze. She didn't plan this: once pleasant
Sunday walk now somber, crowded
like the semi-darkness of a concert hall.

THE FEVERED ARCHAEOLOGISTS

Soon after starting, the scattered
hooves dropped, clubs polished clean
against the sand and clinging to a tightened
fist. This was distance. Twelve years
overseas, half-eaten by provisions,
teething in their tropic cloud.
We shook back, raged against the split
ground, clean catastrophe of gradual
geologic consequence.

DIDAC

Didac is bathing with the door open; burnt
umber under water and his prick upright,
bearded by bubbles.

Grinning he rubs his belly,
lisping Catalonia nativity
as we listen from the kitchen

half looking, half turned back
to see the scurry of a Spanish rat.
He wraps a pregnant pause

with pink and porous revelation.
In tandem we crane our necks,
check the shaking of a cup or

cramped trouser. Yes
Spain is slipping, the language
hides me from your kitchen banter,

bides its time in operatic windows.
The bookshelf stacked and dropping
vowels like unripe apples at my door.

SHE GUNS THE MORNING RIDE

Her mouth is nothing, scored in some
crudely cut amethyst bracelet.

The train's rocking pointedly
described the curves of her left sphenoid,

where she keeps your name. Her rare batted lashes
droop. She takes her pen, afraid of twisting

upward, tipping through the chin, this nib.
She's not concerned with her cardigan

admired by men at the last station, or with
the yolk-streaked dreams she has

nodding off at the window. Jostled
by this keepsake engine. She wipes

a salt drop from her chin and
trails vexed through paper tunnels.

WHAT TEETH KEEP IN THEIR CAVITIES

A country club mint. Its sugar crushed
between the black fingers of a bibliophile.

How laundry smells, or how it feels to climb
inside the cover of a duvet, adjust its corners.

The lip's loose skin, the skin of a boy, we once tasted
in daycare. Steeped gunpowder, pepper pasta.

What being poor does to a communist.
A buried pet, pushing salt up through the lips.

The geranium's warped, well-scrubbed choral singing,
plague boils imagined too often.

The first time stumped by a gentle slap or stupor of
    glass
and Cadillac belt tangle. Ashtray gum, coffee-burned
    tongue

and the smell of the girl behind the counter at a waffle
house. Arthur Rackham's egg-white forehead

shrivelled by the too-fast-turned page. How tongs could
   have
dragged us from the womb, or how we broke our nose,
   twice.

The too-fast talking, two dry choked syllables,
we whistled through the dirge of a drill.

EL LISSITZKY

Recognized now as king he settled
on Helvetica. Had escaped the siege of German
bans, become gradually accustomed to the clean
geometry of high modern zeal.

He bridged the South, learned the native
beauty of the line, tribes that could attack
their young, compelled to solve the problems
of the North, diagonal axis decidedly wise.

The black, red, white wedged and difficult
to read, would be the new palace walls.
He carried campaigns of discontent, promoted
the slope of rank, ignored the past.

Lament for an Outdated Printing Press

In a manner of ceremony, doubtless
about the grave, painted frown
and slightly hard of hearing, they fix
this printed Caslon through a press,
copper in their stools, canoeing
through a Vandercook, all nostalgia
and new tobacco proclamations:
the oak is understated, primping
dab of ink is tacky, straps an eye
across the page, lets it go, unloaded.

SCAVENGER OF SHIPS

Gone mad at sea I followed the clock, exposed
ankle of age. We snuggled, courted the martyrs
of our bedtime stories. It wasn't the quiet sway,

nor the oysters, torn in half, that drove me.
It was the clock, bloody despot, mad-eyed, she fought,
dragged backwards, the bitch kicked,

winced and was frayed like a belt. Gnawed through
I used her to stave off boredom for an hour,
a year. It isn't easy letting stained skin down

gently. I tore my clothes and choked.
The tip of my tongue a lovely blue, I licked
her ear like Claudius and wouldn't let go.

INACCURATE OBSERVATIONS IN CUERNAVACA

Men generally dressed in ponchos,
raised influence of pewter crests marked
like cattle in their Spanish haze.

Breeches, pretty girls like jingles
chiming in a riot, drunk and zealous, scarcely
thinking of the mule, steady load of heavy hatchets.

All primed and gently parting at the clasp. Some say
they press the blades abreast like suckling babes,
pass the blood with milk and mutton through a field.

Imminence spurs a shag of undergrowth to foam
and fill the throat with buzzing hymns, ballads,
bread, rum, young prodigies of labour,

favoured by the coca, upward preening stocks
of law. Immediacy of this clean torso
bare and plastered through the greenery.

THINKING SHE'S POSEIDON

Drinking stone softly she laughed, another
cigarette lit and stubbed for posterity, the sober
glint of light, open strike against the port mirror.

She was losing her girth, linen with embroidered
cock brawls, pink and crimson could not contain
her nosebleeds, nor the ingrown eyelash batting

snug against the sails. Seven days she'd been trapped
tugging oars beneath deck, still twelve weeks to shore,
the bulging gulps of sea, her skin less and less like brass.

THE HOG'S SNOUT IS SOVEREIGN

Saddled by instinct to the centre of the flame
while other scraps, salted by a hoof, boil, fume, harden
white and pink. Wiltshire smoked and granted
a tract of land as wide as footprints brushed to form
the pit, rushed to square away the scent of brine,
rasping thrills of butter crust and jealous embers
unattended. What came next was whining,
tongue-burned oil for a spot of gravy, then hushed
was the snout, timed perfectly to grunt and comfort
with familiar vowels. It opened, split the teeth to quiet,
and licked the wayward wood.

Sarah Miles

Cherub-shawled, hobbling forward
and stitched back with cobble tripping,
too lean the heels; high and tapered, nearly

snapping. She means to keep
these fleeting stones in check, ten steps
to the bridge, thirty to the high climb, arched

entrance of a steeple, shouldered by the
breeze, the abstinent advance
of crows strutting, seasoned in their evening

rigor mortis. The path inadequate against these pillars,
steep ascent or sinking of the stomach, the pews tremor,
organ-struck and gleaming beneath her tight-bent knees.

PROBLEMS OF A PSYCHIC DETECTIVE

At the window, plump afternoon,
remote scene of murder. We studied
the shadows, unfinished sentences, now caked
in blood, in water, they were the syllables

we'd predicted. The language of tradition,
voices stumbling over a name, then
the word, exhausted by our recitation,
was a ghost who, in his English

confidence, unearthed the first fragment:
drizzle, mannish sweep across
the landing signifies this arrogant smirk, or
how obvious the attributes of old remarks.

This foreign education, punctual distaste
for crystal, cards, or for the gentle coaxing
of a hand. Indistinguishable we strip
the past of hazard.

LADY HAMLET AT BRUNCH

Hinges have been known
in ancient times to act the urgency
of honoured house guests,

who, wiping doors and locks, come
to thwart rumours. The copper bed,
obligation of a word, scandal

of a woman in the dark month
of opium and stale tea. Pale
sloping porcelain on her lips,

the gaping cruelty of strangers. She was
a simple re-enactment, the stonemason,
chisel of cold air at the autumn stairs,

frankly speaking. Nothing would
have turned their interests. They were
an antiquated crowd, glass-wrapped

and cloudy. She was the host
of unmeasured mixtures, cold,
noble and drunk with poison.

ALBRECHT DÜRER

Grazed by an inch the arrow passes first
as though its aim suspended
pulls a streak parabola and flees.

A canvas explains nothing, only folds
and musters light. Paint as eager
as a draft is tapered, turpentine

and long evenings spent in composition: inept.
If likeness is won in battle,
the colonel's hands gallop,

fain the reverie of making marks,
expanding left, accepting gods in ruler,
shade, camera obscura. What is there to mimic?

Hooves in pyramidal range flicker in and
out and hold the page's haze, as the painter
holds his infantry at bay.

Angels Caught Later in a Cave

Under his tutorship we filtered out, took
the oracle's daring lifted brow to mean
we would succeed.

Ten days, twelve months and doubled
over where rags required fickle stitching
to unravel.

We lost our sleeves, shoulders spread
to cracking, hastened to control the turning
valley mud-wrung and wounded by our spears.

Being mixed of mind, informal now,
we took to camp, withdrew the infant wings,
feathered tumours still too raw, too cruxed for flight.

We menaced, leaping here and there, as if
to circumvent the sky's guilty hordes: all bright,
pushing us to march.

CHOKED BY THE DEBATE

Insult gave him Babylon, promptly across
the room, nimble they came, argued for the garden's
hanging, snaring vines, could not be swayed.
This was the come-along pivot of discourse, whereby
the sign commits, adept at changing trains, tradition.

The company, being bored, remarked on his absence,
the opposing trespass of his eyes: four glass arches
glazed with moss clinging faraways. They had pushed
too hard with words, had passed him through the well-
     groomed
lip, pressed objects to rank with denotation like the
     verb,
the bird classified by back pattern or by beak.

He'd pardoned the complaints, bypassed
the pleading sovereign grit, only to be replaced,
complacently, by the syrinx.

THE HYMNS OF OLD CREAM GOWNS

Glossed with olive, lost in all the favours of a grouse,
or worse, a spider curt and pining for the lips, the lifted
hems of shepherd girls. Here we learned the rhyme.

Breadcrumbs, loose threads banished through the wood.
The axe that turns lifted at the neck, or oven crisp with
gut threads battered in a pleasant cannibal's cast iron.

Or the lines of Rackham's wildcats and hogs
whose open flanks are filtered out on platters,
        grinning.

HE WANTED A CIGARETTE AT THE DANUBE

The imprint of a three-man tribe,
weed-wrapped and churning, sparks
a ripple. Calls the eye to narrow, stare
from a dim-lit bridge. We see

them as if on screen, rush of light,
shadowed once by a ferry,
once again by the low
passing of a crane, they plead,

press the skulls of soldiers to a stone,
crush their spears through the pelvis
of a girl lifted, held vertically, tipping
till it splits a wave, teeters out of sight.

How They Are Detained

Dirty orange orangutans skelter the island, a blur,
faces broken by a streak of cedar arched above
the entrance, thatch fastened twine-wise to a cage.
Straight-wood palms a longhouse, parts the upper
jaw, gently gnawing day from its inhabitants. The
    clouds
are empty. Want to take the time, tie the eyes
with crows to the weight of going old.
Brush has thickened, rich with drifting flora, awkward
where the forest meets the fleeting of a hare or
bearskin; now stripped and hung slow-cooking
on a stone. The two girls are quarrelling. The younger,
drunk on something handpicked and offered
on a plate of copper clay, has broken, weeps for brick,
silk and for the warmth of marriage, or else cold
    comfort
of a funeral parlour. She is stumbling, sick, slightly
severed. Nail is raw, now more gnawed on
once and eyed by a boy: legless.

SINGING

Teeth are parcels, beads
the painted centre of a song.
Hud, hud, huddle the duck, headless
in a tropic epilogue, woeful at the tongue's
half moon, all mink, mackerel
and earlobe.

There is sympathy in the mouth, incremental,
not to eat, devour, but to graze, soft-
tongued at the sweetness of a cheek
or pepper-knee.

SUSTENANCE

Not the sting, the brewing
seeds, not new split skin –
draining, can detain them.
Parched blows against
the tongue, how thirst
can loosen ties, pry back
the coat's thin weight, change
the face. They bury bits
of self, nails black and
dropping off like apricot.

Cooking Frozen Meat

He slipped between the homemade,
halftone squeak of the calendar,

the advancing covers, cold country air,
irksome tundra bouncing lengthwise

up the spine. It was an old house, habitual
in meaning, rearing up the rival genius son.

Inclined by mirrors to graze or humble snatched
by the thief's fixed stare, the onion in a peach

sink drawing salt down his cheek,
he could not make them proud. The grand

piano he struck for over twenty-seven years
still not right.

FABLE IN THE BUSY MIND

There's nothing lethal in it. Wolves acquired
in their single-file trot against the courtyard,
harried stretch of slowly coming into focus.

Deer shot, scattered boy with shoes too big,
bragging too strangely, how one tackles oak,
disarm the choir's mezo-blades, direct its song to flattery.

Stepping back, the land seems spoken for.
It bluffs its mountains, banter of sheep herd
with her terracotta sheath of breathing soft,

the plain yet watchful contours of her face.
When wanting this we were dissolved, led
cavalry through the brush with a wink.

WHAT WAS LEARNED IN GRADE SCHOOL

A faint voice phlegms loose, and moving
with a new romantic charm, reveals gravity.

Sun passes hill back
into the pines, and curiosity is met

with knowing, mispronounced hopefully
or assumed erroneous blemish.

Buildings will fall. Opinions bid and sway
together like a clique of bullies.

Nothing is assured, only is, and sometimes
takes to courtesy to hide what vein and tendril

slinks beneath us – weary.

We Will Not Count the Words

Thunder's cabin with tin procession slates itself
against the stenciled get-gone figures in the mind,

dry sand, spider-creviced stone, a wiped
mouth knows its place, knows

unfolding in a stymied vowel will shush
the weather, make reluctance bite the cork, rouse

the chairs to itch and lift their tight-lipped fannies
from a stoop. Death without discomfort,

chunks of cedar damp with odours, slow to burn
and sick with indignation.

STEENBUCK

for instance, stumbles gaunt and saunters
nostalgic for the bushman's old assumptions.
How his bow would fold or split apart
and little steeds would follow,
too gentle, two backward glancing
doe eyes fixed prettily upon the barrel, daring.
One would hit the arm, one hidden woman
would chance to find the star's blade fall
and settle split upon the skin.

THE LION-HUNTING MUTT

He would sleep by their cages, encourage
the faded coats to jet out parted by the bars.
He learned fast, a gunned deterrent

from deer or jackrabbit, to strike, recover
clubbed overtures with subtle shaking tail.
You can't unnerve the hound, wide dirge

of fang, at a moment more heavy; canyon-struck,
he'd shoot out strained, before the pack, slip
and stumble cliff-wise past his prey.

DIANE

Distracted from the features, tucked hubris
with a strain of sibling rouse, she struck him.

Big game, big grunt Orion, with his new star suit
of curving winter over cottages and tents.

She hauled the sky, Scorpio stretched and kept
averted, felt extinction in a glint-marred cloud.

Unending clock backed up about the bowline knot.
A blade connecting the surface to its source.

Cherry with the thrill of spilling out recovered.
She could not die.

Pretty mouth, a thousand iris stamps, one face,
she rests at the gate, an illustration.

MUSEUM OF NATURAL HISTORY

A glacier begins its preservation
of a coat. Coral misplacement
of each early hub

moving often, moving close against
the open minds of early excavators.
Must find the China boar

to mount, let little girls and fickle
students smooth the surface
with a glance.

Flourish with light, ivy, mink
and modern forest portraits
of a bloated leaf. Equator splits, we sit

drifting through her scientific
recollections. Must learn the globe,
notice the sea floor's steady spreading

out, dismantled. Lava keeps them,
caves, glacial spillage keeps
them folded neat and buzzing.

THE TAXIDERMIST'S DAUGHTER

A handful of rabbits sniff the northern
loads, scuttle new and steadied in
their reinvention. It takes a foot

to fortune. Wood to keep the marble
eyes in place – three fingers, collar
sullied, cigarettes while wide

awake and sowing. Each body she
finds, she charms. Heat kept and
frankincense. Smoke may rise, paper

out about how strange these
barefaced twisting yarns.
Though by the end she made them

breathe. Family of unthroated carnival
birds, chinchilla, short-tempered tree
lizards or a toad.

Guard his broken neck, tie him through
a pillow, leaf-embroidered,
safely stitched away.

THE MYTH OF HEALING

Struma tumours bloat, returning
to touch. The king's damnedest cured
by coins and soldiers hunched like rigs
unfurling. Necks swollen, customary

words translated through palm
or fingertip. Patience, you conquistadors;
these are cures. Buzzards hum, the pillars
standing watch, unflinching. Charged in the arrest

of being stone. Recharging we recount, as if we
knew, the citadel's slow whistle into night.
How the droves would filter out – breathing,
stinted by the cold, the shrinking throats.

Feet, Small and Shapely

Compose the mud, rove in clusters through
calamities of packed and stranded minnows.

Fought was the instinct to slip a toe
through, to crush a silver streak forgiven.

Light snickers, shaves the sprouting faces
with an apricot abandon.

Know your knife, show the gods
your canteen's brimming lid.

Each regular wave of harbour baited,
hooked and lowered to a seeming crack of fury.

Fish go hungry to the victor. Menaced jerks of sand
sloping cleft about the rubber boots,

then resting stern to dry and flake, lean behind
the coaxed disciples, boys whose maple trousers

snag and thread about the blossom's dirge.
They must be earnest, rather zested with the dewless

walls of summer cabins. A year is steeped, a bloom
is ruthless when the bar's at stake,

steady rising in a high campaign of casting out,
catching something wide and writhing, greater than the
    self.

FISTS AND DOLLARS AND ALL THAT

A chest takes gambits. Mouths
with ale for brass take air and slug
it through new threats like vengeful
trollops.

Misstep, clinging to the saddle.
Round the heel, tilt
the digging spade, lifted lip,
proud new scar, pussing gums,

squint or smarmy,
full-grown beard and fearful only
when the dimples close. Fish bone;
a toothpick, smoke; the horseman's

lung and loosened morals. Make
caskets silhouettes. March in lonely
swagger to the red dirt's rattlesnake
incisions.

Best shot, best from far away and still
you hit the noose. Keep noose knot from
neck and heathens from the margin
of a needing town.

What's Left of a Sunday Afternoon

Casual, the pigeon takes his place
amongst the ruins. Doting flocks circle
overhead, cursing as if stone
could hear them. Sunday

is a rivet, bolts cloud to weed and past
to the quiet of a scene. See the king
lean back thinking of the virgin's lips.
Noose tightened with each touch. Or

of cherry pickers, scuffed mirrors, the way
the walls once seemed to close in round
a milkmaid's morning banter. The cavalries,
reduced to nail and bone and buried in the cliffs.

Even the worms they fed have passed.
Now there's only the morning pigeon,
rind of muddied copper on the loft.

EXILED MONARCH

Migrained in an asphalt slip, she counts
the voices by the door. Gravity becomes
her; sunk sockets, chalk complexion.
She turns to music. Something
low enough to wrap the toes, violins pass
chipped bronze polish, press like fingers
to her soles. Beneath, the skin's a shrine,

mind, windless standing over cliffs,
an effigy. She won't fold. Furnishes
her vanity with stones, soldiers smooth
to stroke when down. She'll hug
the chimney's heat as if it were a king,
cling, half sleeping, to her salt duvet.

DOUBTFUL, DUTIFUL

Clavicle, unaccustomed to the touch, prompts
an altar boy to twist his zipper. Bride is twenty-five,
sings off-key a psalm she wants to come to feet,

frock itself in flesh, halt the whole procession.
Heels heavy, gauzed in taffeta, face painted
by the light of stained-glass cavalries. Easy is the slip,

cream clean across her waist, the way she paces aisles,
wrinkles at the whisper of a front-pew parson,
his slacks spread, head cocked to draw her back

in thought. The organ's low pipes stretched
along the walls, old waltzes heavy, so she splits
as she approaches, says I do.

ACKNOWLEDGEMENTS

I would like to acknowledge the generous financial assistance of the Toronto Arts Council.

Thank you to the editors of the following journals, who published poems from this collection: *CV2*, *Misunderstandings Magazine*, *The Toronto Quarterly*, *The Puritan*, *Dandelion*, *All Rights Reserved*, *Berkeley Poetry Review*, *The Cortland Review* and *The Westchester Review*.

Thank you to everyone who has influenced and supported me: Sheri Richardson, Fred Richardson, Dave Richardson, Lee and Henri, Sean Stanley, Selena Cristo-Williams, Kate Knapp Johnson, Daniel Long, Matthea Harvey, Stephen Dobyns, Suzanne Gardinier, Susan Hoover, Kevin Connolly, Suzanne Buffam and Kevin Pilkington.

Paul Vermeersch and Jeramy Dodds, your editorial input, encouragement and guidance have been invaluable. I know how lucky I've been.

I would also like to acknowledge the random bits of literature, art and film culture that pop up in these poems: *Mrs Beeton's Book of Household Management*, Zane Grey, Colin Wilson, Arthur Rackham, Albrecht Dürer, Graham Greene, Virginia Woolf, Katharine Hepburn, Clint Eastwood, Sergio Leone and El Lissitzky.